2016 NACWE Prayer Call
Handouts

2016 NACWE Prayer Call Handouts, Copyright 2017 by National Association of Christian Women Entrepreneurs (NACWE)

Scripture quotations marked (NIV) are taken from the Holy Bible, New International Version®, NIV®. Copyright © 1973, 1978, 1984, 2011 by Biblica, Inc.™ Used by permission of Zondervan. All rights reserved worldwide. www.zondervan.com The "NIV" and "New International Version" are trademarks registered in the United States Patent and Trademark Office by Biblica, Inc.™

Scripture quotations marked (ESV) are from The ESV® Bible (The Holy Bible, English Standard Version®), copyright © 2001 by Crossway, a publishing ministry of Good News Publishers. Used by permission. All rights reserved."

All NACWE prayer call handouts were inserted in their original format, which accounts for various inconsistencies throughout the book.

RHEMA Publishing House.™
rhemapublishinghouse.com
PO Box 1244 McKinney, TX

ISBN: 978-0-9990932-4-5

Welcome to the Soul of NACWE!

The National Association of Christian Women Entrepreneurs (NACWE) has always been known for its heart, and we want to formally introduce you to our prayer and devotion corner, the Soul of NACWE. Our sisterhood is here to support you on your personal journey of faith and how that is intertwined with your business. We believe in the transforming power of prayer.

- **We pray daily for our Members**
- **We pray together weekly in a special Members call**
- **We hand out a weekly Prayer Call guide, and we offer these to you in this booklet.**

In our businesses, God is our CEO.

For Members of the National Association of Christian Women Entrepreneurs, Devotion to God comes first and we are reminded of the acrostic: **J - O - Y**

    J stands for Jesus—He comes first.
    O stands for others—they come next.
    Y stands for yourself—and in this group, your Entrepreneurial endeavors!

Jesus First: *"But seek first the kingdom of God and his righteousness, and all these things will be added to you."* Matthew 6:33

Others Next: *"As each has received a gift, use it to serve one another, as good stewards of God's varied grace…"* 1 Peter 4:10

Your Work: *"Commit your work to the Lord, and your plans will be established."* Proverbs 16:3

        LEADERS AND MEMBERS IN NACWE ARE COMMITTED
        AND DEDICATED TO GOD AND HIS WAYS.

Thank you to all who have led us in these endeavors by managing, leading, writing, and praying; you are SO dear to us!
 -Barbara Hollace, Sally Adamcik, Marian Struble, Diane Cunningham, Karen Lindwall- Bourg, and Courtenay Blackwell
 -and all participating NACWE Members

Prayer Calls 2016

Faith	*1*
Hope	*2*
Love	*3*
Speaking	*4*
Courage	*5*
Wisdom	*6*
Writing	*7*
Commitment	*8*
Strength	*9*
Wait	*10*
Listen	*11*
Go	*12*
Vision	*13*
Grace	*14*
Pereverance	*15*
Gratitude	*16*
Trust	*17*
Ask	*18*
Seek	*19*
Knock	*20*
Teamwork	*21*
Message	*22*
Truth	*23*
Integrity	*24*
Teaching	*25*
Boldness	*26*
Majesty/Majestic	*27*
Remember	*28*

Worth/Worthy	29
Freedom	30
Self-Control	31
Stewardship	32
Victory	33
Cost	34
Communication	35
Instruction(s)	36
Effort	37
Excellent/Excellence	38
Heart	39
Life/Life-Giving	40
Plans	41
Questions	42
Actions	43
Obedience	44
Triumph	45

NACWE PRAYER CALL   February 4, 2016
FAITH

One of the characteristics that make NACWE unique is that we are women of faith. We are the National Association of <u>Christian</u> Women Entrepreneurs. Our discussion and prayer time this week will focus on FAITH. You can call in and just listen or participate in the discussion as you feel led to do so. We will spend the last part of the call in prayer, silently or out loud.

You are a woman of great faith ~ you are a Christian woman entrepreneur. You are loved.

SCRIPTURE:

Faith is confidence in what we hope for and assurance about what we do not see.
Hebrews 11:1 (NIV)

Knowing that the testing of your faith produces endurance. James 1:3 (NASB)

Because you have so little faith. I tell you this: *if you had even a faint spark of faith*, even faith as *tiny as* a mustard seed, you could say to this mountain, "Move from here to there," and *because of your faith*, the mountain would move. *If you had just a sliver of faith*, you would find nothing impossible. Matthew 17:20 (VOICE)

For we walk by faith, not by sight.   2 Corinthians 5:7 (ESV)

QUOTE: "Faith is taking the first step even when you don't see the whole staircase."
~ Martin Luther King, Jr.

DISCUSSION:

1. How is your faith reflected in your business?

2. Have you taken a leap of faith in a new area in 2016?

PRAYER: Open for prayer requests.

© 2016 National Association of Christian Women Entrepreneurs * All Rights Reserved * www.nacwe.org

NACWE PRAYER CALL   February 11, 2016
HOPE

One of the characteristics that makes NACWE unique is we are the National Association of <u>Christian</u> Women Entrepreneurs. You are a woman of great faith ~ you are a Christian woman entrepreneur. There is hope in the name of the Lord. Always remember, you are loved.

SCRIPTURE:

But now, Lord, what do I look for? My hope is in you. Psalm 39:7 (NIV)

Blessed be the God and Father of our Lord Jesus Christ! According to his great mercy, he has caused us to be born again to a living hope through the resurrection of Jesus Christ from the dead. 1 Peter 1:3 (NIV)

Not only so, but we also glory in our sufferings, because we know that suffering produces perseverance; 4 perseverance, character; and character, hope. 5 And hope does not put us to shame, because God's love has been poured out into our hearts through the Holy Spirit, who has been given to us. Romans 5:3-5 (NIV)

May the God of hope fill you with all joy and peace in believing, so that by the power of the Holy Spirit you may abound in hope. - Romans 15:13 (NIV)

QUOTE: Hope is faith holding out its hand in the dark. ~George Iles

DISCUSSION:

    1. Is hope one of the intangibles that you offer your clients?

    2. As an entrepreneur, how do you fuel hope in your own life?

PRAYER: Open for prayer requests.

© 2016 National Association of Christian Women Entrepreneurs * All Rights Reserved * www.nacwe.org

NACWE PRAYER CALL   February 18, 2016
LOVE

One of the characteristics that makes NACWE unique is we are the National Association of <u>Christian</u> Women Entrepreneurs. You are a woman of great faith ~ you are a Christian woman entrepreneur. Jesus loves YOU... this I know for the Bible tells me so. You are loved!

SCRIPTURE:

A friend loves at all times and a brother is born for a time of adversity. **Proverbs 17:17** (NIV)

Jesus said to him, 'You shall love the LORD your God with all your heart, with all your soul, and with all your mind.' This is the first and great commandment. And the second is like it: 'You shall love your neighbor as yourself.' **Matthew 22:37–39** (NKJV)

Greater love has no one than this, that he lay down his life for his friends. **John 15:13** (NIV)

Love is patient, love is kind. It does not envy, it does not boast, it is not proud. It is not rude, it is not self-seeking, it is not easily angered, it keeps no record of wrongs. Love does not delight in evil but rejoices with the truth. It always protects, always trusts, always hopes, always perseveres. Love never fails ... **1 Corinthians 13: 4-8a** (NIV)

QUOTE: Spread love everywhere you go. Let no one ever come to you without leaving happier.
– Mother Teresa

DISCUSSION:
1. How do you continue to keep your "love" of being an entrepreneur fresh in your heart?

2. What are some tangible ways you can "love" yourself? (self-care)

PRAYER: Open for prayer requests.

© 2016 National Association of Christian Women Entrepreneurs * All Rights Reserved * www.nacwe.org

NACWE PRAYER CALL   February 25, 2016
SPEAKING

One of the characteristics that makes NACWE unique is we are the National Association of <u>Christian</u> Women Entrepreneurs. You are a woman of great faith ~ a Christian women entrepreneur. You have a message to share. God puts the words inside of you and empowers you to speak clearly and with boldness. Then He calls us to speak the message He has given.

SCRIPTURE:

The good person out of the good treasure of his heart produces good, and the evil person out of his evil treasure produces evil, for out of the abundance of the heart his mouth speaks. **Luke 6:45** (ESV)

Be very careful, then, how you live—not as unwise but as wise, making the most of every opportunity, because the days are evil. Therefore do not be foolish, but understand what the Lord's will is. Do not get drunk on wine, which leads to debauchery. Instead, be filled with the Spirit, speaking to one another with psalms, hymns, and songs from the Spirit. Sing and make music from your heart to the Lord, always giving thanks to God the Father for everything, in the name of our Lord Jesus Christ. **Ephesians 5:15-20** (NIV)

Now go; I will help you speak and will teach you what to say. **Exodus 4:12** (NIV)

QUOTE: Speak in such a way that others love to listen to you. Listen in such a way that others love to speak to you. -Anonymous

DISCUSSION:
1. How do you make sure the treasures of your heart and therefore your words are good?

2. What one or two word/sentence message has God given you that you could share today?

PRAYER: Open for prayer requests.

© 2016 National Association of Christian Women Entrepreneurs * All Rights Reserved * www.nacwe.org

NACWE PRAYER CALL   March 3, 2016
COURAGE

One of the characteristics that makes NACWE unique is we are the National Association of <u>Christian</u> Women Entrepreneurs. You are COURAGEOUS! You are a Christian woman entrepreneur.

SCRIPTURE:

Have I not commanded you? Be strong and courageous. Do not be afraid; do not be discouraged, for the LORD your God will be with you wherever you go." Joshua 1:9 (NIV)

Wait for the LORD; Be strong and let your heart take courage; Yes, wait for the LORD. Psalm 27:14 (NASB)

These things I have spoken to you, so that in Me you may have peace. In the world you have tribulation, but take courage; I have overcome the world. John 16:33 (NASB)

QUOTE: "Success is not final, failure is not fatal: it is the courage to continue that counts." – Winston Churchill

DISCUSSION:
1. What makes you more courageous or what eats away at your courage?

PRAYER: Open for prayer requests.

© 2016 National Association of Christian Women Entrepreneurs * All Rights Reserved * www.nacwe.org

NACWE PRAYER CALL   March 10, 2016
WISDOM

One of the characteristics that makes NACWE unique is we are the National Association of <u>Christian</u> Women Entrepreneurs. Wisdom is the gift that King Solomon sought above all others. I pray that pursuing wisdom is our high calling as well.

SCRIPTURE:

If any of you lacks wisdom, you should ask God, who gives generously to all without finding fault, and it will be given to you. James 1:5 (NIV)

For the Lord gives wisdom; from his mouth come knowledge and understanding. Proverbs 2:6 (NIV)

Be very careful, then, how you live—not as unwise but as wise, making the most of every opportunity, because the days are evil. Ephesians 5:15-16 (NIV)

I keep asking that the God of our Lord Jesus Christ, the glorious Father, may give you the Spirit of wisdom and revelation, so that you may know him better. Ephesians 1:17 (NIV)

QUOTE: "Wisdom is not a product of schooling but of the lifelong attempt to acquire it." ~ Albert Einstein

DISCUSSION:
    1. Wisdom is what we learn from the mistakes of others. Knowledge is what we learn by making our own mistakes. Where are you along this spectrum? Still learning by making your own mistakes or learning wisdom from others including your NACWE sisters?

PRAYER: Open for prayer requests.

© 2016 National Association of Christian Women Entrepreneurs * All Rights Reserved * www.nacwe.org

NACWE PRAYER CALL   March 17, 2016

WRITING

One of the characteristics that makes NACWE unique is we are the National Association of <u>Christian</u> Women Entrepreneurs. You are a Christian woman entrepreneur with something to say. Whether you are writing your business plan, a blog, a book, the words have been written in your heart by the Author of Life. You have a message....Your story entwined with His Story!

SCRIPTURE:

"My heart is stirred by a noble theme as I recite my verses for the king; my tongue is the pen of a skillful writer." ***Psalm 45:1***

"Then the LORD answered me and said, "Record the vision And write it on tablets, That the one who reads it may run. 3"For the vision is yet for the appointed time; It hastens toward the goal and it will not fail. Though it tarries, wait for it; For it will certainly come, it will not delay...." **Habukkuk 2:2,3**

QUOTE: Fill the paper with the breathings of your heart. William Wordsworth

DISCUSSION:

1. How has/does writing strengthened your walk with God?
2. How has your writing impacted you or someone else?

PRAYER: Open for prayer requests.

© 2016 National Association of Christian Women Entrepreneurs * All Rights Reserved * www.nacwe.org

NACWE PRAYER CALL   March 24, 2016
COMMITMENT

One of the characteristics that makes NACWE unique is we are the National Association of <u>Christian</u> Women Entrepreneurs. We are only a few days away from Easter, and Jesus shows us the ultimate picture of commitment as He endured the cross for our sins that we might have eternal life with Him.

SCRIPTURE:

And may your hearts be fully committed to the LORD our God, to live by his decrees and obey his commands, as at this time." 1 Kings 8:61(NIV)

Commit everything you do to the LORD. Trust him, and he will help you. Psalm 37:5 (NLT)

And Jesus, crying out with a loud voice, said, "Father, INTO YOUR HANDS I COMMIT MY SPIRIT." Having said this, He breathed His last. Luke 23:46 (NASB)

QUOTE: "There's a difference between interest and commitment. When you're interested in something, you do it only when it's convenient. When you're committed to something, you accept no excuses; only results." - Kenneth Blanchard

DISCUSSION: How has commitment played a role in your life as an entrepreneur?

PRAYER: Open for prayer requests.

NACWE PRAYER CALL   March 31, 2016
STRENGTH

One of the characteristics that makes NACWE unique is we are the National Association of <u>Christian</u> Women Entrepreneurs. We all have days when we need greater strength. The Lord offers a never-ending supply. So grateful for His amazing grace.

SCRIPTURE:

God is our refuge and strength, an ever-present help in times of trouble. Psalm 46:1 (GOD'S WORD)

I can do ALL things through Christ who strengthens me. Philippians 4:13 (NKJV)

But those who wait on the Lord shall renew their strength; they shall mount up with wings like eagles, they shall run and not be weary, they shall walk and not faint. Isaiah 40:31 (NKJV)

QUOTE: "Be faithful in small things because it is in them that your strength lies." ~ Mother Teresa

DISCUSSION: In your business, how have you turned a weakness into a strength?

PRAYER: Open for prayer requests.

© 2016 National Association of Christian Women Entrepreneurs * All Rights Reserved * www.nacwe.org

NACWE PRAYER CALL   April 7, 2016
WAIT

One of the characteristics that makes NACWE unique is we are the National Association of <u>Christian</u> Women Entrepreneurs. Often God asks us to wait on Him to receive the blessings He has for us. Waiting isn't easy but it's worth it! Let's wait together for Him in prayer.

SCRIPTURE:

Therefore the LORD longs to be gracious to you, And therefore <u>He waits</u> on high to have compassion on you. For the LORD is a God of justice; How blessed are all those who long for Him. Isaiah 30:18 (NASB)

Rest in the LORD and <u>wait patiently</u> for Him; Do not fret because of him who prospers in his way, Because of the man who carries out wicked schemes. Psalm 37:7 (NASB)

And while staying with them he ordered them not to depart from Jerusalem, but to <u>wait for the promise</u> of the Father. Acts 1:4 (RSV)

QUOTE: "Waiting ... the most difficult part of hope." – Unknown

DISCUSSION: What are you waiting for – in either your business or your personal life? Why?

PRAYER: Open for prayer requests.

© 2016 National Association of Christian Women Entrepreneurs * All Rights Reserved * www.nacwe.org

NACWE PRAYER CALL   April 14, 2016
LISTEN

One of the characteristics that makes NACWE unique is we are the National Association of <u>Christian</u> Women Entrepreneurs. Listening ~ we miss so much when we don't listen to each other or to our heavenly Father. Stop. Wait. Listen. Then Obey.

SCRIPTURE:

Listen to advice and accept instruction, that you may gain wisdom in the future.
~Proverbs 19:20 (ESV)

Then you will call on me (God) and come and pray to me, and I will listen to you.
~Jeremiah 29:12 (NIV)

My dear brothers and sisters, take note of this: Everyone should be quick to listen, slow to speak and slow to become angry. ~James 1:19 (NIV)

QUOTE:
"To listen well is as powerful a means of communication and influence as to talk well."
– John Marshall

DISCUSSION: In your business, if you were to assign percentages to the amount of time that you listen to your clients versus the amount of time you speak to your clients, what would those percentages be?

PRAYER: Open for prayer requests.

© 2016 National Association of Christian Women Entrepreneurs * All Rights Reserved * www.nacwe.org

NACWE PRAYER CALL   April 21, 2016

GO

One of the characteristics that makes NACWE unique is we are the National Association of <u>Christian</u> Women Entrepreneurs. You are a woman of great faith ~ you are a Christian woman entrepreneur~you are called by God to Go into the world He has given you and shine for Him. He never calls without equipping and has given you all you need to carry out that mission effectively.

SCRIPTURE:

For as the rain and snow come down from heaven and do not return there but water the earth, making it bring for the sprout, giving seed to the sower and bread to the eater, so shall my word be that goes out from my mouth; it shall not return to me empty, but it shall accomplish that which I purpose, and shall succeed in the thing for which I sent it. For you shall go out in joy, and be led forth in peace; the mountains and the hills before you shall break forth into singing, and all the trees of the field shall clap their hands.......and it shall make a name for the Lord. Isaiah 55:10-13

The in inhabitants of one city will go to another, saying, "Let us go at once to entreat the favor of the Lord and seek the Lord of hosts; I myself am going." Zechariah 8:21

Arise and let us go up against them, for we have seen the land, and behold it is very good. And you you will do nothing? Do not be slow to go, to enter and possess the land. Judges 18:9

QUOTE: Go confidently in the direction of your dreams. Live the life you have imagined. Henry David Thoreau

DISCUSSION:

© 2016 National Association of Christian Women Entrepreneurs * All Rights Reserved * www.nacwe.org

NACWE PRAYER CALL   May 5, 2016
VISION

One of the characteristics that makes NACWE unique is we are the National Association of <u>Christian</u> Women Entrepreneurs. Vision ~ God has unique ideas for each of us. This month's NACWE theme is events, may God give you the vision to fulfill your purpose in His kingdom. Today is National Day of Prayer in the United States.

SCRIPTURE:

One night the Lord spoke to Paul in a vision and told him, "Don't be afraid! Speak out! Don't be silent!" Acts 18:9 (NLT)

Where there is no vision, the people perish: but he that keeps the law, happy is he. Proverbs 29:18 (AKJV)

Then the LORD answered me and said, "Record the vision and inscribe it on tablets, that the one who reads it may run. For the vision is yet for the appointed time; it hastens toward the goal and it will not fail. Though it tarries, wait for it; for it will certainly come, it will not delay." Habakkuk 2:2-3 (NASB)

QUOTE: "The only thing worse than being blind is having sight but no vision."
– Helen Keller

DISCUSSION: Has God given you an idea or a vision for your business/ministry? If so, have you acted on it? If not, what's the first step you need to take?

PRAYER: Open for prayer requests.

© 2016 National Association of Christian Women Entrepreneurs * All Rights Reserved * www.nacwe.org

NACWE PRAYER CALL   May 12, 2016
GRACE

One of the characteristics that makes NACWE unique is we are the National Association of <u>Christian</u> Women Entrepreneurs. Amazing grace how sweet the sound that saved a wretch like me, I once was lost but now I'm found was blind but now I see.

SCRIPTURE:

Three times I pleaded with the Lord to take it away from me. But he said to me, "My grace is sufficient for you, for my power is made perfect in weakness." Therefore I will boast all the more gladly about my weaknesses, so that Christ's power may rest on me. **2 Corinthians 12:8-9 (NIV)**

Let us then with confidence draw near to the throne of grace, that we may receive mercy and find grace to help in time of need. **Hebrews 4:16 (ESV)**

See to it that no one fails to obtain the grace of God; that no "root of bitterness" springs up and causes trouble, and by it many become defiled. **Hebrews 12:15 (ESV)**

QUOTE: "What gives me the most hope every day is God's grace; knowing that his grace is going to give me the strength for whatever I face, knowing that nothing is a surprise to God." – Rick Warren

DISCUSSION: How is "God's grace" a part of your business on a daily basis? Regarding your clients? Your colleagues? Yourself?

PRAYER: Open for prayer requests.

© 2016 National Association of Christian Women Entrepreneurs * All Rights Reserved * www.nacwe.org

NACWE PRAYER CALL   May 19, 2016
PERSEVERANCE

One of the characteristics that makes NACWE unique is we are the National Association of <u>Christian</u> Women Entrepreneurs. As an entrepreneur, we are called to persevere because the road isn't easy. As believers, Jesus told us we would have tribulation but to be of good cheer, because Christ has overcome the world!

SCRIPTURE:

Therefore, since we are surrounded by such a great cloud of witnesses, let us throw off everything that hinders and the sin that so easily entangles. And let us run with perseverance the race marked out for us. **Hebrews 12:1 (NIV)**

Blessed is the one who perseveres under trial because, having stood the test, that person will receive the crown of life that the Lord has promised to those who love him. **James 1:12 (NIV)**

Not only that, but we also <u>rejoice</u> in our sufferings, because we know that suffering produces perseverance; perseverance, character; and character, hope. **Romans 5:3-4 (Berean Study Bible)**

QUOTE: "Everything I've ever been able to accomplish in skating and in life has come out of adversity and perseverance." – Scott Hamilton

DISCUSSION: In our discussion today, we have seen that there is a 'reward' for persevering. Share an example of when this happened in your life or your business.

PRAYER: Open for prayer requests.

© 2016 National Association of Christian Women Entrepreneurs * All Rights Reserved * www.nacwe.org

NACWE PRAYER CALL   May 26, 2016
GRATITUDE

One of the characteristics that makes NACWE unique is we are the National Association of <u>Christian</u> Women Entrepreneurs. You are a woman of great faith ~ you are a Christian woman entrepreneur. Seeing yourself, others and your business through eyes of Gratitude, can change everything.

SCRIPTURE:

The one who offers thanksgiving (gratitude) as his sacrifice glorifies me; to one who orders his way rightly I will show the salvation of God. **Psalm 50:23**

At that time his voice shook the earth, but now he has promised, "Yet once more I will shake not only the earth but also the heavens." This phrase, "Yet once more," indicates the removal of things that are shaken, that is things that have been made, in order that the things that cannot be shaken may remain. Therefore let us be grateful for receiving a kingdom that cannot be shaken, and let us offer to God acceptable worship, with reverence and awe, for our God is a consuming fire. **Hebrews 12:26-29**

Do not be anxious about anything, but in everything by prayer and supplication with thanksgiving (gratitude) let your requests be made known to God. And the peace of God , which surpasses all understanding, will guard your hearts and your minds in Christ Jesus. Whatever is true, whatever is honorable, whatever is just, whatever is pure, whatever is lovely, whatever is commendable, if there is any excellence if there is anything worthy of praise, think about these things. **Phillipians 4:6-8**

QUOTE: Gratitude bestows reverence....changing forever how we experience life and the world.

John Milton

DISCUSSION:

1. What is your favorite way to express gratitude?

PRAYER: Open for prayer requests.

© 2016 National Association of Christian Women Entrepreneurs * All Rights Reserved * www.nacwe.org

NACWE PRAYER CALL   June 2, 2016
TRUST

One of the characteristics that makes NACWE unique is we are the National Association of <u>Christian</u> Women Entrepreneurs. As you do the work God has for you, you will need a team. We are called to be trustworthy as team members and as the leader, to trust God and others to help us fulfill our mission.

SCRIPTURE:

Trust in the Lord with all your heart and lean not on your own understanding; in all your ways submit to him, and he will make your paths straight. **Proverbs 3:5-6 (NIV)**

But select capable men from all the people –men who fear God, trustworthy men who hate dishonest gain – and appoint them as officials over thousands, hundreds, fifties and tens. **Exodus 18:21 (NIV)**

Some trust in chariots and some in horses, but we trust in the name of the LORD our God. **Psalm 20:7 (NIV)**

QUOTE: "Your faithfulness makes you trustworthy to God." ~Edwin Louis Cole

DISCUSSION: Do find it challenging to trust others to help you carry out your vision?

PRAYER: Open for prayer requests.

© 2016 National Association of Christian Women Entrepreneurs * All Rights Reserved * www.nacwe.org

NACWE PRAYER CALL   June 9, 2016
ASK

One of the characteristics that makes NACWE unique is we are the National Association of <u>Christian</u> Women Entrepreneurs. Asking for help is often our wisest choice but also our greatest difficulty. There is no shame in asking for help. God wants to help you in your personal life and your business. He is always on call.

SCRIPTURE:

When Moses' father-in-law saw all that Moses was doing for the people, he asked, "What are you really accomplishing here? Why are you trying to do all this alone while everyone stands around you from morning till evening?" **Exodus 18:14-15 (NLT)**

When all your people Israel pray and ask for help, as they acknowledge their intense pain and spread out their hands toward this temple, then listen from your heavenly dwelling place, forgive their sin, and act favorably toward each one based on your evaluation of their motives. (Indeed you are the only one who can correctly evaluate the motives of all people.) Then they will honor you by obeying you throughout their lifetimes as they live on the land you gave to our ancestors. **2 Chronicles 6:29-31 (NET)**

If you need wisdom, ask our generous God, and he will give it to you. He will not rebuke you for asking. **James 1:5 (NLT)**

QUOTE: "Some people think God does not like to be troubled with our constant coming and asking. The way to trouble God is not to come at all." - Dwight L. Moody

DISCUSSION: Are you quick to ask for help or only as a last resort?

PRAYER: Open for prayer requests.

NACWE PRAYER CALL   June 16, 2016
SEEK

One of the characteristics that makes NACWE unique is we are the National Association of <u>Christian</u> Women Entrepreneurs. Being an entrepreneur involves seeking, taking action. This includes not only finding team members and clients, but seeking the Lord's calling for us in our business and in the world.

SCRIPTURE:

"But seek first His kingdom and His righteousness, and all these things will be added to you. **Matthew 6:33 (NASB)**

When you seek me in prayer and worship, you will find me available to you. If you seek me with all your heart and soul, I will make myself available to you,' says the Lord. **Jeremiah 29:13-14a (NET)**

Seek the LORD and His strength; Seek His face continually. **1 Chronicles 16:11 (KJV)**

QUOTE: "Most people seek after what they do not possess and are enslaved by the very things they want to acquire." – Anwar Sadat (former President of Egypt)

DISCUSSION: What are you seeking today that seems elusive to you, in either your business or your personal life?

PRAYER: Open for prayer requests.

© 2016 National Association of Christian Women Entrepreneurs * All Rights Reserved * www.nacwe.org

NACWE PRAYER CALL   June 23, 2016
KNOCK

One of the characteristics that makes NACWE unique is we are the National Association of <u>Christian</u> Women Entrepreneurs. You are a woman of great faith ~ a Christian women entrepreneur. You need open doors. Doors to wisdom, strategy, and people's needs and hearts. God understands knocking. It was His idea in the first place. Come let us reason together and pray.

SCRIPTURE:

"Look! I stand at the door and knock. If you hear my voice and open the door, I will come in, and we will share a meal together as friends. **Rev. 3:20 NLT**

"You're out of your mind," they told her. When she kept insisting that it was so, they said, "It must be his angel." **16** But Peter kept on knocking, and when they opened the door and saw him, they were astonished. **17** Peter motioned with his hand for them to be quiet and described how the Lord had brought him out of prison. "Tell James and the other brothers and sisters about this," he said, and then he left for another place. **Acts 12:15-17 New International Version (NIV)**

"Be dressed for service and keep your lamps burning, **36** as though you were waiting for your master to return from the wedding feast. Then you will be ready to open the door and let him in the moment he arrives and knocks. **Luke 12:35-37 NLT**

QUOTE: The Lord is knocking on the door of our hearts. Have we put a sign out that says, "Do Not Disturb."   Pope Francis

DISCUSSION:

1. What are you knocking on the door of God's heart for?

2. What is He knocking on your door about?

PRAYER: Open for prayer requests.

© 2016 National Association of Christian Women Entrepreneurs * All Rights Reserved * www.nacwe.org

NACWE PRAYER CALL   June 30, 2016
TEAMWORK

One of the characteristics that makes NACWE unique is we are the National Association of <u>Christian</u> Women Entrepreneurs. Often we are called to work together to achieve God's purpose in our lives and effect change in our world. We are better together.

SCRIPTURE:

As iron sharpens iron, so one person sharpens another. **Proverbs 27:17 (NIV)**

God has shown you His grace in many different ways. So be good servants and use whatever gift He has given you in a way that will best serve each other. **1 Peter 4:10 (ERV)**

For the body is not one member, but many. **1 Corinthians 12:14 (KJV)**

QUOTE: "Alone we can do so little, together we can do so much." – **Helen Keller**

DISCUSSION: What is holding you back from adding the next person to your team?

PRAYER: Open for prayer requests.

© 2016 National Association of Christian Women Entrepreneurs * All Rights Reserved * www.nacwe.org

NACWE PRAYER CALL   July 6, 2016
MESSAGE

One of the characteristics that makes NACWE unique is we are the National Association of <u>Christian</u> Women Entrepreneurs. What is the message you are trying to convey? Whether it is about your business, your faith or your life, share what's on your heart.

SCRIPTURE:

For this is the message you have heard from the beginning: We must love one another. **1 John 3:11 (NIV)**

Get up and go to the great city of Nineveh and deliver the message I have given you. **Jonah 3:2 (ERV)**

But the Lord stood at my side and gave me strength, so that through me the message might be <u>fully proclaimed</u> and all the Gentiles might hear it. And I was delivered from the lion's mouth. **2 Timothy 4:17 (NIV)**

QUOTE: "Every happening, great and small, is a parable whereby God speaks to us, and the art of life is to get the message." ~ Malcom Muggeridge

DISCUSSION: We each have a unique message to share. Name one creative way to share your message. Name a fear that is holding you back.

PRAYER: Open for prayer requests.

NACWE PRAYER CALL   July 14, 2016
TRUTH

One of the characteristics that makes NACWE unique is we are the National Association of <u>Christian</u> Women Entrepreneurs. You are a woman of great faith ~ a Christian women entrepreneur. Personally and corporately, we come together to grow in truth, face the truth, speak the truth, and live the truth as we grow deeper in relationship with the One Who Is the Truth! We are blessed.

SCRIPTURE:

James 1:18 Of his own will he brought us forth by the word of truth, that we should be a kind of first fruits of his creatures.

Zechariah 8:16 These are the things that you shall do: Speak the truth to one another; render in your gates judgments that are true and make for peace;

John 8:31-32 … So Jesus said to the Jews who had believed in him, "If you abide in my word, you are truly my disciples, and you will know the truth, and the truth will set you free."

Ephesians 4:25 Therefore, having put away falsehood, let each one of you speak the truth with his neighbor, for we are members one of another.

QUOTE: The truth doesn't cost anything, but a lie could cost you everything.

DISCUSSION:
1. What truth has God been revealing to you?
2. How could that truth impact your business or your circle of influence?

PRAYER: Open for prayer requests.

© 2016 National Association of Christian Women Entrepreneurs * All Rights Reserved * www.nacwe.org

NACWE PRAYER CALL   July 21, 2016
INTEGRITY

One of the characteristics that makes NACWE unique is we are the National Association of <u>Christian</u> Women Entrepreneurs. Integrity is what makes us shine from the inside, out. It is vital we are a living example to our clients of the difference between the world and the standards of a believer.

SCRIPTURE:

The integrity of the upright will guide them, but the crookedness of the treacherous will destroy them. **Proverbs 11:3 (NASB)**

Show yourself in all respects to be a model of good works, and in your teaching show integrity, dignity, and sound speech that cannot be condemned, so that an opponent may be put to shame, having nothing evil to say about us. **Titus 2:7-8 (ESV)**

For the LORD gives wisdom; from his mouth come knowledge and understanding; he stores up sound wisdom for the upright; he is a shield to those who walk in integrity, guarding the paths of justice and watching over the way of his saints. **Proverbs 2:6-8 (ESV)**

QUOTE: "Few things are more infectious than a godly lifestyle. The people you rub shoulders with everyday need that kind of challenge. Not prudish. Not preachy. Just Cracker Jack clean living. Just honest to goodness, bone – deep, non-hypocritical integrity." ~ **Chuck Swindoll**

DISCUSSION: Integrity is vital in our business and personal life. In your experience, has integrity even been an issue in your business dealings?

PRAYER: Open for prayer requests.

NACWE PRAYER CALL   July 28, 2016
TEACHING

One of the characteristics that makes NACWE unique is we are the National Association of <u>Christian</u> Women Entrepreneurs. Teaching what we know to this generation and generations yet to come is a mandate from God. What are you doing to share your legacy in both your business and personal life?

SCRIPTURE:

Now, go! I myself will help you with your speech, and I'll teach you what you are to say." ~**Exodus 4:12 (ISV)** (God talking to Moses)

Let the message about Christ, in all its richness, fill your lives. Teach and counsel each other with all the wisdom he gives. Sing psalms and hymns and spiritual songs to God with thankful hearts. ~ **Colossians 3:16 (NLT)**

A student is no better than his teacher. But everyone who is well-trained will be like his teacher. ~ **Luke 6:40 (God's WORD)**

QUOTE: Good teachers know how to bring out the best in students." ~ Charles Kuralt

DISCUSSION: Teaching is sharing what we know. Is teaching a regular part of your business? Should it be?

PRAYER: Open for prayer requests.

NACWE PRAYER CALL   August 11, 2016
BOLDNESS

One of the characteristics that makes NACWE unique is we are the National Association of <u>Christian</u> Women Entrepreneurs. Boldness means the quality of standing out strongly and distinctly. That's who we are, bold women sharing the love of Jesus in our lives, our homes, and our business. Be BOLD as a lion!

SCRIPTURE:

Let us therefore draw near with boldness unto the throne of grace, that we may receive mercy, and may find grace to help us in time of need. ~ **Hebrews 4:16 (ESV)**

The wicked flee though no one pursues, but the righteous are as bold as a lion. ~ **Proverbs 28:1 (NIV)**

And pray for me, too. Ask God to give me the right words so I can boldly explain God's mysterious plan that the Good News is for Jews and Gentiles alike. I am in chains now, still preaching this message as God's ambassador. So pray that I will keep on speaking boldly for him, as I should. ~ **Ephesians 6:19-20 (NLT)**

QUOTE: "Prayer in private results in boldness in public." ~ Edwin Louis Cole

DISCUSSION: Being bold isn't always easy. Is there an area in your life where you need boldness?

PRAYER: Open for prayer requests.

© 2016 National Association of Christian Women Entrepreneurs * All Rights Reserved * www.nacwe.org

NACWE PRAYER CALL   August 18, 2016
MAJESTY/MAJESTIC

One of the characteristics that makes NACWE unique is we are the National Association of <u>Christian</u> Women Entrepreneurs. Nature is filled with His majesty. He is majestic in all the earth. Worship His Majesty!

SCRIPTURE:

Yours, Lord, is the greatness and the power and the glory and the **majesty** and the splendor, for everything in heaven and earth is yours. Yours, Lord, is the kingdom; you are exalted as head over all. ~ **1 Chronicles 29:11 (NIV)**

Lord, our Lord, how **majestic** is your name in all the earth! – **Psalm 8:9 (NIV)**

To the only wise God our Savior, be glory and **majesty**, dominion and power, both now and ever. Amen. ~ **Jude 1:25 (KJV)**

QUOTE: "To have God speak to the heart is a majestic experience, an experience that people may miss if they monopolize the conversation and never pause to hear God's responses." ~ Charles Stanley

DISCUSSION: We see evidence of God in all creation. What are some ways you capture and appreciate the Majesty of God in your life?

PRAYER: Open for prayer requests.

© 2016 National Association of Christian Women Entrepreneurs * All Rights Reserved * www.nacwe.org

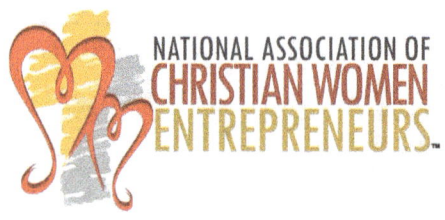

NACWE PRAYER CALL   August 25, 2016
REMEMBER

One of the characteristics that makes NACWE unique is we are the National Association of <u>Christian</u> Women Entrepreneurs. It's important to remember what God has done in your life and your business. He is faithful, never forget that. He never forgets you.

SCRIPTURE:

When I send clouds over the earth, the rainbow will appear in the clouds, and I will remember my covenant with you and with all living creatures. Never again will the floodwaters destroy all life. When I see the rainbow in the clouds, **I will remember** the eternal covenant between God and every living creature on earth."
 ~**Genesis 9:14-16 (NLT)**

Yet I still dare to hope when I **remember** this: The faithful love of the Lord never ends! His mercies never cease. Great is his faithfulness; his mercies begin afresh each morning. I say to myself, "The Lord is my inheritance; therefore, I will hope in him!"
~**Lamentations 3:21-24 (NLT)**

After Jesus was raised from the dead, his followers **remembered** that Jesus had said this. Then they believed the Scripture and the words Jesus had said.
~ **John 2:22 (NCV)**

QUOTE: "Every great dream begins with a dreamer. Always remember, you have within you the strength, the patience, and the passion to reach for the stars to change the world." ~ **Harriet Tubman**

DISCUSSION: What is one positive trait about yourself that you need to remember on the days when life is hard, your business is slow, and your finances need a boost?

PRAYER: Open for prayer requests.

© 2016 National Association of Christian Women Entrepreneurs * All Rights Reserved * www.nacwe.org

NACWE PRAYER CALL   September 1, 2016
WORTH/WORTHY

One of the characteristics that makes NACWE unique is we are the National Association of <u>Christian</u> Women Entrepreneurs. God is worthy of our praise! We are created in His image. He died for us. We have great worth in His sight.

SCRIPTURE:

Great is the Lord and most **worthy** of praise; his greatness no one can fathom.
~ **Psalm 145:3 (NIV)**

Indeed, the very hairs of your head are all numbered. Don't be afraid; you are **worth** more than many sparrows. ~ **Luke 12:7 (NLT)**

To this end we also pray always for you, that our God may count you **worthy** of your calling, and fulfill every desire of goodness and work of faith, with power.
~ **2 Thessalonians 1:11 (World English Bible)**

QUOTE: "Don't worry when you are not recognized, but strive to be **worthy** of recognition." ~ **Abraham Lincoln**

DISCUSSION: Have you ever struggled with your "worth" and how that translates to what you charge your clients? How did you overcome this obstacle?

PRAYER: Open for prayer requests.

© 2016 National Association of Christian Women Entrepreneurs * All Rights Reserved * www.nacwe.org

NACWE PRAYER CALL   September 8, 2016
FREEDOM

One of the characteristics that makes NACWE unique is we are the National Association of <u>Christian</u> Women Entrepreneurs. Freedom ~ our country was founded on the concept. We are free in Christ. Yet, freedom has a lot of responsibility that comes with it as well as great reward.

SCRIPTURE:

The Spirit of the LORD is upon me, because the LORD has anointed me; he has sent me to bring good news to the oppressed and to bind up the brokenhearted, to proclaim freedom for the captives, and release from darkness for the prisoners.
~ **Isaiah 61:1 (ISV)**

Now the Lord is the Spirit, and where the Spirit of the Lord is, there is freedom.
~ **2 Corinthians 3:17 (NIV)**

For you have been called to live in freedom, my brothers and sisters. But don't use your freedom to satisfy your sinful nature. Instead, use your freedom to serve one another in love. For the whole law can be summed up in this one command: "Love your neighbor as yourself." ~ **Galatians 5:13-14 (NLT)**

QUOTE: "Freedom means the opportunity to be what we never thought we would be."~ **Daniel Boorstin**

DISCUSSION: Being an entrepreneur is often perceived as having the freedom to do what we want to do, when we want to do it. How has that concept played out in your business? What are the obstacles to "freedom" you have faced?

PRAYER: Open for prayer requests.

© 2016 National Association of Christian Women Entrepreneurs * All Rights Reserved * www.nacwe.org

NACWE PRAYER CALL   September 15, 2016
SELF-CONTROL

One of the characteristics that makes NACWE unique is we are the National Association of <u>Christian</u> Women Entrepreneurs. Self-control... we often talk about it in relation to our diet, but it affects every area of our lives. May we be Holy Spirit-controlled... we are to daily die to self and be made a new creation in Him.

SCRIPTURE:

A person without **self-control** is like a city with broken-down walls.
~ **Proverbs 25:28 (NLT)**

But the fruit of the Spirit is love, joy, peace, forbearance, kindness, goodness, faithfulness, gentleness and **self-control.** Against such things there is no law.
~**Galatians 5:22-23 (NIV)**

Be sober and **self-controlled**. Be watchful. Your adversary, the devil, walks around like a roaring lion, seeking whom he may devour.
~ **1 Peter 5:8 (World English Bible)**

QUOTE: "God has equipped you to handle difficult things. In fact, He has already planted the seeds of discipline and **self-control** inside you. You just have to water those seeds with His Word to make them grow!" ~ **Joyce Meyer**

DISCUSSION: Is there one area in your *business* where you struggle with self-control? (You fill in the blank.) (I will offer some examples on our Thursday call.

PRAYER: Open for prayer requests.

© 2016 National Association of Christian Women Entrepreneurs * All Rights Reserved * www.nacwe.org

NACWE PRAYER CALL   September 22, 2016
STEWARDSHIP

One of the characteristics that makes NACWE unique is we are the National Association of Christian Women Entrepreneurs. You are a woman of great faith ~ a Christian women entrepreneur. God has given you ideas, talents, finances, gifts, relationships and everything within you to make a difference and honor Him. It is up to you how you steward and take care of what you have been given. A good and faithful steward will be given more to steward.

SCRIPTURE:
1 Corinthians 4:1-2
Let a man regard us in this manner, as servants of Christ and stewards of the mysteries of God. In this case, moreover, it is required of stewards that one be found trustworthy.

1 Peter 4:10-11
As each one has received a special gift, employ it in serving one another as good stewards of the manifold grace of God. Whoever speaks, is to do so as one who is speaking the utterances of God; whoever serves is to do so as one who is serving by the strength which God supplies; so that in all things God may be glorified through Jesus Christ, to whom belongs the glory and dominion forever and ever. Amen.

Colossians 1:24-29

Now I rejoice in my sufferings for your sake, and in my flesh I do my share on behalf of His body, which is the church, in filling up what is lacking in Christ's afflictions. 25 Of this church I was made a minister according to the stewardship from God bestowed on me for your benefit, so that I might fully carry out the preaching of the word of God, 26 that is, the mystery which has been hidden from the past ages and generations, but has now been manifested to His saints, 27 to whom God willed to make known what is the riches of the glory of this mystery among the Gentiles, which is Christ in you, the hope of glory. 28 We proclaim Him, admonishing every man and teaching every man with all wisdom, so that we may present every man complete in Christ. 29 For this purpose also I labor, striving according to His power, which mightily works within me.

QUOTE: "Stewardship is caring for what belongs to God. It is rooted in a recognition that everything we have is from God and everything we have is God's." Bernard F. Evans

DISCUSSION:

1. What obstacles do you face in maintaining good stewardship?

2. How has being a good steward affected your business or your life?

PRAYER: Open for prayer requests.

© 2016 National Association of Christian Women Entrepreneurs * All Rights Reserved * www.nacwe.org

NACWE PRAYER CALL   September 29, 2016
VICTORY!

One of the characteristics that makes NACWE unique is we are the National Association of <u>Christian</u> Women Entrepreneurs. We have victory in Jesus no matter our circumstances. Sometimes we are called to persevere before the victory arrives. Don't give up!

SCRIPTURE:

For the LORD your God is going with you! He will fight for you against your enemies, and He will give you **victory**! ~ **Deuteronomy 20:4 (NLT)**

A horse is prepared for the day of battle, but **victory** comes from the LORD.
~ **Proverbs 21:31 (Holman Christian Standard Bible)**

For everyone who has been born of God overcomes the world. And this is the **victory** that has overcome the world—our faith. ~ **1 John 5:4 (ESV)**

QUOTE: "Only God can turn a mess into a message, a test into a testimony, a trial into a triumph and a victim into a victory."~ **Anonymous**

DISCUSSION: Often through our toughest moments we learn our greatest lessons, what lesson have you learned where victory was clothed in what looked like defeat?

PRAYER: Open for prayer requests.

© 2016 National Association of Christian Women Entrepreneurs * All Rights Reserved * www.nacwe.org

NACWE PRAYER CALL   October 6, 2016
COST

One of the characteristics that makes NACWE unique is we are the National Association of <u>Christian</u> Women Entrepreneurs. You are a woman of great faith ~ a Christian women entrepreneur. The plans God has for you in every area of life and business did not come without great cost to Jesus. Your service to others sometimes comes at great cost too. Thankfully, we never need run out of resources as long as we come to His infinite supply that is freely given without cost!

SCRIPTURE:

Psalm 15:5 (MSG) "Keep your word even when it costs you, make an honest living,
  never take a bribe.

1 Corinthians 6:20 and 7:33 You have been bought, and at what a price! Therefore bring glory to God both in your body and your spirit, for they both belong to him. …… You have been redeemed, at tremendous cost; don't therefore sell yourselves as slaves to men! My brothers, let every one of us continue to live his life with God in the state in which he was when he was called.

Luke 14:28 For which one of you, when he wants to build a watchtower [for his guards], does not first sit down and calculate the cost, to see if he has enough to finish it?

QUOTE: "A sacrifice to be real must cost, must hurt, and must empty ourselves. Give yourself fully to God. He will use you to accomplish great things on the condition that you believe much more in his love than in your weakness." Mother Teresa

DISCUSSION:

1. What, other than money, has being a Christian Entreprenuer cost you?
2. What process or action do you take when you are evaluating the non-monetary costs of achieving your goals or dreams?

PRAYER: Open for prayer requests.

NACWE PRAYER CALL   October 13, 2016
COMMUNICATION

One of the characteristics that makes NACWE unique is we are the National Association of <u>Christian</u> Women Entrepreneurs. Communication is critical in every area of our lives. What are you trying to communicate through your marketing message? What message are your people actually receiving? God hears the cries of our heart… yes, this is communication as well.

SCRIPTURE:

Let the words of my mouth and the meditation of my heart be acceptable in your sight, O LORD, my rock and my redeemer. ~ **Psalm 19:14 (ESV)**

Like apples of gold in settings of silver is a word spoken in right circumstances. ~ **Proverbs 25:11 (NASB)**

Let no corrupt communication proceed out of your mouth, but that which is good to the use of edifying, that it may minister grace unto the hearers. ~ **Ephesians 4:29 (KJV)**

QUOTE: "The most important thing about communication is hearing what isn't said." ~ **Peter Drucker**

DISCUSSION: Communication is the vehicle we use in sales and marketing to convey our message. Can you name one facet of communication you struggle with?

PRAYER: Open for prayer requests.

© 2016 National Association of Christian Women Entrepreneurs * All Rights Reserved * www.nacwe.org

NACWE PRAYER CALL   October 20, 2016
INSTRUCTION/INSTRUCTIONS

One of the characteristics that makes NACWE unique is we are the National Association of <u>Christian</u> Women Entrepreneurs. Are you good at following instructions? The Lord often led His people by giving them instructions and then expecting they would follow them. For us, as well as our clients, it can still be a struggle to follow the instruction manual.

SCRIPTURE:

Then the Lord said to Moses, "I will rain down bread from heaven for you. The people are to go out each day and gather enough for that day. In this way I will test them and see whether they will follow my **instructions**." ~ **Exodus 16:4 (NIV)**

Hold on to **instruction**, do not let it go; guard it well, for it is your life.
~ **Proverbs 4:13 (NIV)**

Go out and preach the word! Go whether it's an opportune time or not! Reprove, warn, and encourage; *but do so* with all the patience and **instruction** *needed to fulfill your calling* because a time will come when some will no longer tolerate sound teaching. Instead, they will live by their own desires; they'll scratch their itching ears by surrounding themselves with teachers who *approve of their lifestyles and* tell them what they want to hear. ~ **2 Timothy 4:2-3 (VOICE)**

QUOTE: "Photograph: a picture painted by the sun without instruction in art."
~ **Ambrose Bierce**

DISCUSSION: As an entrepreneur there are times when we "break the rules" and other times when it's important to follow the instructions. Is there an area where you struggle in following the instructions?

PRAYER: Open for prayer requests.

© 2016 National Association of Christian Women Entrepreneurs * All Rights Reserved * www.nacwe.org

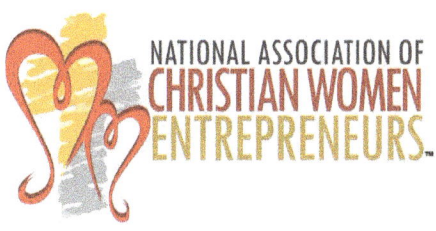

NACWE PRAYER CALL   October 27, 2016
EFFORT

One of the characteristics that makes NACWE unique is we are the National Association of <u>Christian</u> Women Entrepreneurs. There is nothing in the business world that happens without effort. God works with us BUT we need to give it our best effort as well.

SCRIPTURE:

I have given him Egypt as a reward for his **efforts** because he and his army did it for me, declares the Sovereign Lord. ~ **Ezekiel 29:20 (NIV)**

Let us therefore make <u>every</u> **effort** to do what leads to peace and to mutual edification. ~ **Romans 14:19 (NIV)**

For this very reason, make <u>every</u> **effort** to add to your faith goodness; and to goodness, knowledge; and to knowledge, self-control; and to self-control, perseverance; and to perseverance, godliness. ~ **2 Peter 1:5-6 (NIV)**

QUOTE: "We all have dreams. But in order to make dreams come into reality, it takes an awful lot of determination, dedication, self-discipline, and effort."
~ **Jesse Owens** (4 Gold medals @ the 1936 Olympics, his record stood for 25 yrs.)

DISCUSSION: We can attend conferences, listen to webinars and even hire a coach, but knowledge without action will not change our lives or our business. What is one area in your business where you need to step up your effort?

PRAYER: Open for prayer requests.

© 2016 National Association of Christian Women Entrepreneurs * All Rights Reserved * www.nacwe.org

NACWE PRAYER CALL   November 3, 2016
EXCELLENT/EXCELLENCE

One of the characteristics that makes NACWE unique is we are the National Association of <u>Christian</u> Women Entrepreneurs. God calls us to the standard of excellence. That's different than perfection. Excellence is a reflection of God in everything we say and do.

SCRIPTURE:

Then this Daniel became distinguished above all the other presidents and satraps, because an **excellent** spirit was in him. And the king planned to set him over the whole kingdom. ~ **Daniel 6:3 (ESV)**

This is a trustworthy saying. And I want you to stress these things, so that those who have trusted in God may be careful to devote themselves to doing what is good. These things are **excellent** and profitable for everyone.~ **Titus 3:8 (NIV)**

Finally, brothers and sisters, whatever is true, whatever is noble, whatever is right, whatever is pure, whatever is lovely, whatever is admirable—if anything is **excellent** or praiseworthy—think about such things. ~ **Philippians 4:8 (NIV)**

QUOTE: "Be a yardstick of quality. Some people aren't used to an environment where excellence is expected." ~ **Steve Jobs**

DISCUSSION: How do you pursue excellence in your business? In your personal life?

PRAYER: Open for prayer requests.

© 2016 National Association of Christian Women Entrepreneurs * All Rights Reserved * www.nacwe.org

NACWE PRAYER CALL   November 10, 2016
HEART

One of the characteristics that makes NACWE unique is we are the National Association of Christian Women Entrepreneurs. You are a woman of great faith ~ a Christian women entrepreneur. God has placed within your heart His heart for your life, your business, and the world. May we all beat with the rhythm of His heart for us and the world.

SCRIPTURE:
1 Peter 3:3-4 ESV
Do not let your adorning be external—the braiding of hair and the putting on of gold jewelry, or the clothing you wear— but let your adorning be the hidden person of the heart with the imperishable beauty of a gentle and quiet spirit, which in God's sight is very precious.

Psalm 90:12 NIV
Teach us to number our days, that we may gain a heart of wisdom.

Psalm 147:3
He heals the broken hearted and binds up their wounds.

QUOTE: "Of all the music that reached the farthest into heaven is the beating of a loving heart." Henry Ward Beecher.

DISCUSSION:
  1. A heart functions best with good blood flow. Would Flow describe where your life, business, etc is right now? Why or why not?

  2. Where are you experiencing God's heart in your life?

PRAYER: Open for prayer requests.

© 2016 National Association of Christian Women Entrepreneurs * All Rights Reserved * www.nacwe.org

NACWE PRAYER CALL   November 15, 2016
LIFE/LIFE-GIVING

One of the characteristics that makes NACWE unique is we are the National Association of <u>Christian</u> Women Entrepreneurs. God has called us to "live" life to the fullest. Our company culture should be life-giving to ourselves as well as those we serve.

SCRIPTURE:

Then the Lord God formed a man from the dust of the ground and breathed into his nostrils the breath of **life**, and the man became a living being. ~ **Genesis 2:7 (NIV)**

Whoever heeds **life-giving** correction will be at home among the wise.
~**Proverbs 15:31 (NIV)**

In him was **life**, and that **life** was the light of all mankind. ~ **John 1:4 (NIV)**

QUOTE: "My mission in life is not merely to survive, but to thrive; and to do so with some passion, some compassion, some humor, and some style." ~ **Maya Angelou**

DISCUSSION: Does your business environment, your company culture impact the lives of your clients?

Is it life-giving, not only to your customers/clients but to you?

PRAYER: Open for prayer requests.

© 2016 National Association of Christian Women Entrepreneurs * All Rights Reserved * www.nacwe.org

NACWE PRAYER CALL   December 1, 2016
PLANS

One of the characteristics that makes NACWE unique is we are the National Association of <u>Christian</u> Women Entrepreneurs. Plans… it's how our dreams become reality. Flying by the seat of your pants doesn't always work… what are God's plans for you? Search the Scriptures. The Bible is your instruction manual.

SCRIPTURE:

Many are the **plans** in a person's heart, but it is the Lord's purpose that prevails.
~**Proverbs 19:21 (NIV)**

I know the **plans** that I have for you, declares the Lord. They are **plans** for peace and not disaster, **plans** to give you a future filled with hope. ~ **Jeremiah 29:11 (GW)**

Plans fail for lack of counsel, but with many advisers they succeed.
~ **Proverbs 15:22 (NIV)**

QUOTE: "Life is what happens while you are busy making other plans."
~ **John Lennon**

DISCUSSION: What plans do you have for the remainder of 2016? What obstacles keep you from completing your plans?

PRAYER: Open for prayer requests.

NACWE PRAYER CALL   December 8, 2016
QUESTIONS

One of the characteristics that makes NACWE unique is we are the National Association of <u>Christian</u> Women Entrepreneurs. Without asking questions, how do we learn? Questions are what bring a dream to reality. What questions have been asked and answered in 2016?

SCRIPTURE:

When the queen of Sheba heard about the fame of Solomon and his relationship to the Lord, she came to test Solomon with **hard questions**. ~**1 Kings 10:1 (NIV)**

After three days they found him (Jesus) in the temple courts, sitting among the teachers, listening to them and asking them **questions**. ~ **Luke 2:46 (NIV)**

Herod asked Jesus many questions, but Jesus said nothing. ~ **Luke 23:9 (NCV)**

QUOTE: "Questions wake people up. They prompt new ideas. They show people new places, new ways of doing things." ~ **Michael Marquardt**

DISCUSSION: How do questions play a role in your business? Are you afraid to ask yourself or your clients the "hard" questions?

PRAYER: Open for prayer requests.

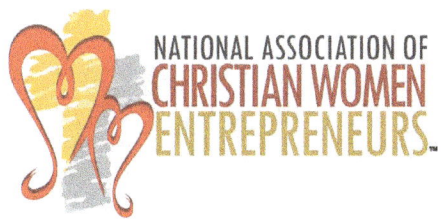

NACWE PRAYER CALL   December 15, 2016
ACTION

One of the characteristics that makes NACWE unique is we are the National Association of <u>Christian</u> Women Entrepreneurs. We often can get stuck in information-gathering mode so that we fail to take action. "Go" is an action word that Jesus used.

SCRIPTURE:

So now transform your ways and **actions**. Obey the Lord your God and the Lord may relent and not carry out the harm that he's pronounced against you.
~ **Jeremiah 26:13 (CEB)**

Moses was educated in all the wisdom of the Egyptians and was powerful in speech and **action**. ~ **Acts 7:22 (NIV)**

For I know your eagerness to help, and I have been boasting about it to the Macedonians, telling them that since last year you in Achaia were ready to give; and your enthusiasm has stirred most of them to **action**.~ **2 Corinthians 9:2 (NIV)**

QUOTE: "For every failure, there's an alternative course of **action**. You just have to find it. When you come to a roadblock, take a detour." ~ **Mary Kay Ash**

DISCUSSION: Which is more challenging for you: to refrain from impetuously taking action or to be so frozen by fear you don't take action? What adjustments do you need to make to your 'default' behavior to overcome this obstacle?

PRAYER: Open for prayer requests.

© 2016 National Association of Christian Women Entrepreneurs * All Rights Reserved * www.nacwe.org

NACWE PRAYER CALL   December 22, 2016
Obedience

One of the characteristics that makes NACWE unique is we are the National Association of <u>Christian</u> Women Entrepreneurs. You are a woman of great faith ~ a Christian women entrepreneur. A woman of Faith understands that her Father loves her and wants the best for her life. She listens and hears His voice and follows His direction.

SCRIPTURE:

Hebrews 5: 7-9 In the days of his flesh, Jesus offered up prayers and supplications, with loud cries and tears, to him who was able to save him from death, and he was heard because of his reverence. 8 Although he was a son, he learned obedience through what he suffered. 9 And being made perfect, he became the source of eternal salvation to all who obey him, 10 being designated by God a high priest after the order of Melchizedek.

<u>2 Corinthians 9:13 (NIV)</u>
This service that you perform is not only supplying the needs of the Lord's people but is also overflowing in many expressions of thanks to God. Because of the service by which you have proved yourselves, others will praise God for the *obedience* that accompanies your confession of the gospel of Christ, and for your generosity in sharing with them and with everyone else.

2 Corinthians 10:4,5
The weapons we fight with are not the weapons of the world. On the contrary, they have divine power to demolish strongholds. 5We demolish arguments and every pretension that sets itself up against the knowledge of God, and we take captive every thought to make it obedient to Christ.

QUOTE: "Obedience is an act of faith; disobedience is the result of unbelief." Edwin Louis Cole

DISCUSSION:
1. When you hear the word Obey or Obedience what are your initial images or thoughts and your emotions around those words? How does that perception influence your obedience?

2. What have you learned about obedience through difficult times?

PRAYER: Open for prayer requests.

© 2016 National Association of Christian Women Entrepreneurs * All Rights Reserved * www.nacwe.org

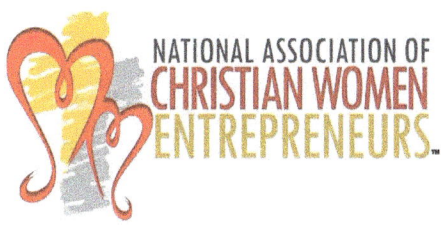

NACWE PRAYER CALL   December 29, 2016
TRIUMPH

One of the characteristics that makes NACWE unique is we are the National Association of <u>Christian</u> Women Entrepreneurs. You are a woman of great faith ~ a Christian women entrepreneur. As 2016 draws to a close, we walk into these final days in triumph because we are daughters of the Most High God.

SCRIPTURE:

You have delivered me from all my troubles, and my eyes have looked in **triumph** on my foes. ~**Psalm 54:7 (NIV)**

But thanks be to God, who in Christ always leads us in **triumph**, and through us spreads the fragrance of the knowledge of him everywhere.
~ **2 Corinthians 2:14 (RSV)**

They (his enemies) will wage war against the Lamb, but the Lamb will **triumph** over them because he is Lord of lords and King of kings—and with him will be his called, chosen and faithful followers." ~ **Revelation 12:11 (NIV)**

QUOTE: "History has demonstrated that the most notable winners usually encountered heartbreaking obstacles before they triumphed. They won because they refused to become discouraged by their defeats." ~ B.C. Forbes

DISCUSSION:

1. As 2016 comes to an end, identify one area where you feel you have been triumphant in your business/ your personal life?

2. According to our quote today, people win because they are not discouraged by their defeats. Name one area of your business where you are trying to overcome an obstacle in 2017.

PRAYER: Open for prayer requests.

© 2016 National Association of Christian Women Entrepreneurs * All Rights Reserved * www.nacwe.org

www.ingramcontent.com/pod-product-compliance
Lightning Source LLC
Chambersburg PA
CBHW080229020526
44113CB00051B/2636